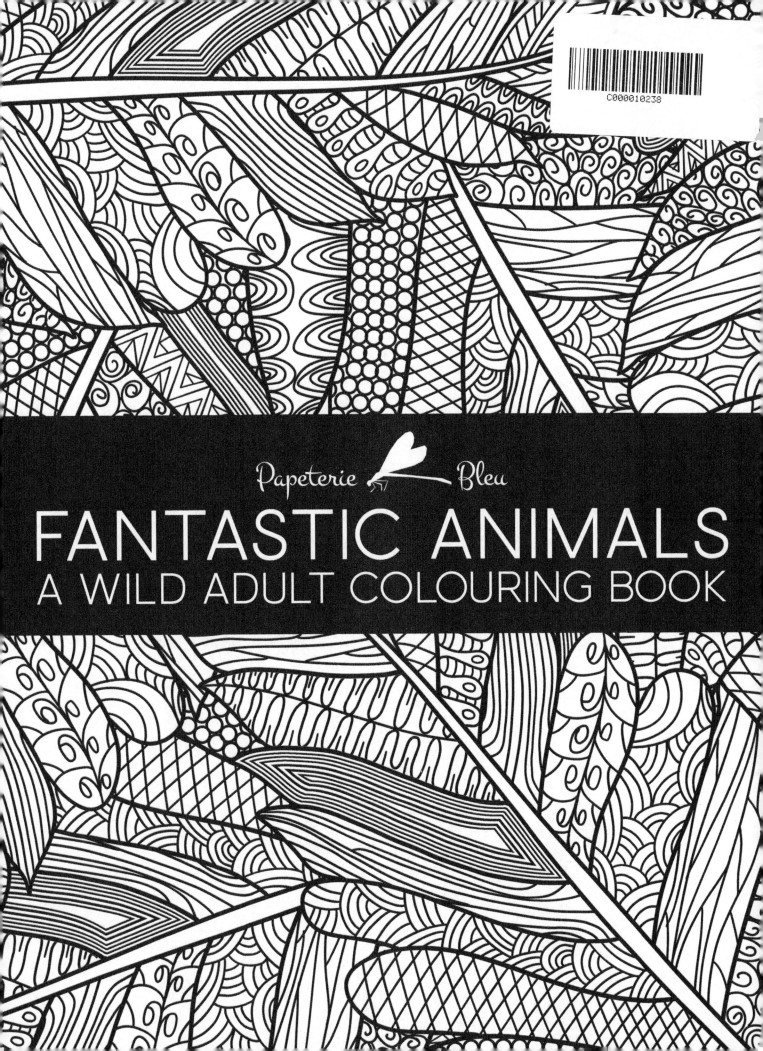

Papeterie Bleu

FANTASTIC ANIMALS
A WILD ADULT COLOURING BOOK

Want free goodies?
Email us at freebies@pbleu.com

@papeteriebleu

Papeterie Bleu

Shop our other books at
www.pbleu.com

Wholesale distribution through Ingram Content Group
www.ingramcontent.com/publishers/distribution/wholesale

For questions and customer service, email us at
support@pbleu.com

FREE PDF DOWNLOAD OF THIS BOOK

www.papeteriebleu.com/animals

YOUR DOWNLOAD CODE: FAN6734

@papeteriebleu

Papeterie Bleu

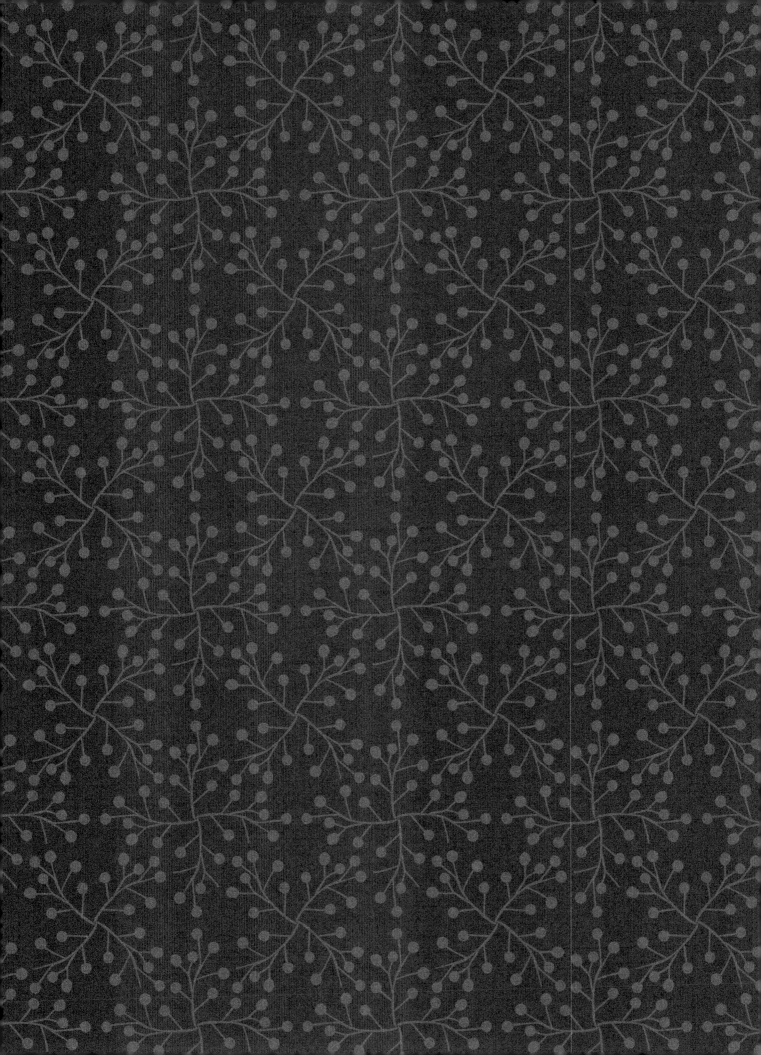

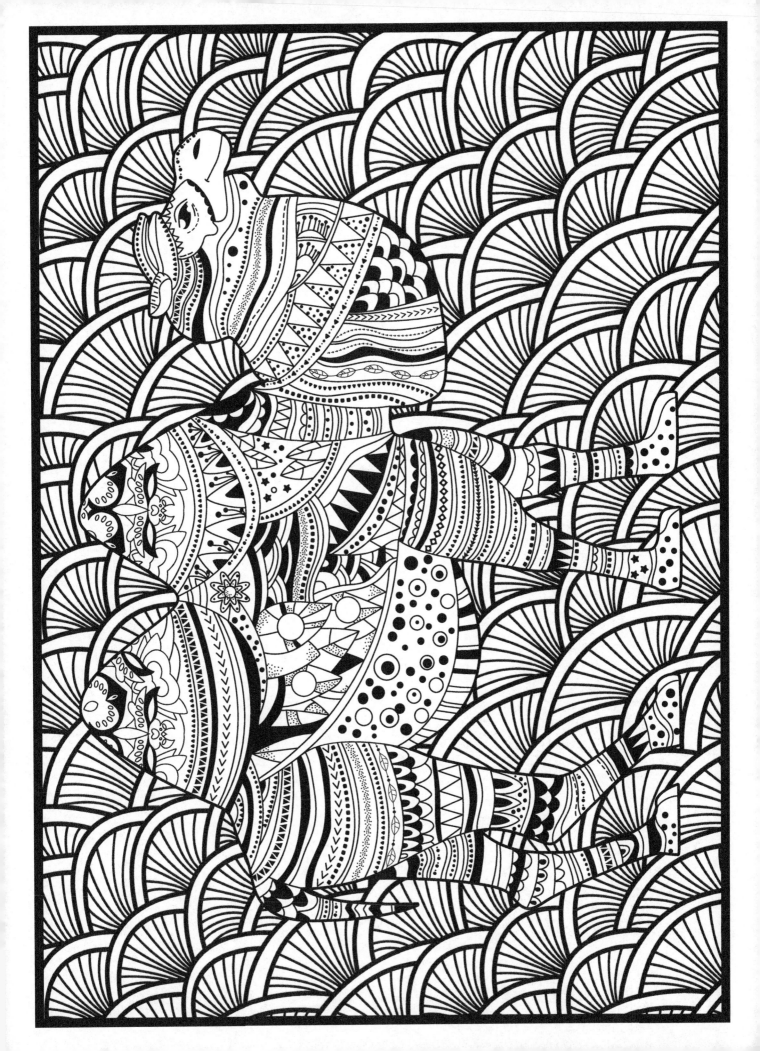

FREE PDF DOWNLOAD OF THIS BOOK

www.papeteriebleu.com/animals

YOUR DOWNLOAD CODE: FAN6734

@papeteriebleu

Papeterie Bleu

Want free goodies?
Email us at freebies@pbleu.com

@papeteriebleu

Papeterie Bleu

Shop our other books at
www.pbleu.com

Wholesale distribution through Ingram Content Group
www.ingramcontent.com/publishers/distribution/wholesale

For questions and customer service, email us at
support@pbleu.com

COLOR TEST PAGE

COLOR TEST PAGE

Printed in Great Britain
by Amazon

27360806R00046